D1607024

How Italian Immigrants Made America Home

How Italian Immigrants Made America Home

LAURA LA BELLA

rosen publishing's
rosen central®

New York

Published in 2019 by The Rosen Publishing Group, Inc.
29 East 21st Street, New York, NY 10010

Cataloging-in-Publication Data

Names: La Bella, Laura, author.
Title: How Italian immigrants made America home / Laura La Bella.
Description: New York : Rosen Central, 2019 | Series: Coming to America: the history of immigration to the United States | Includes bibliographical references and index. | Audience: Grades 5–8.
Identifiers: ISBN 9781508181293 (library bound) | ISBN 9781508181309 (pbk.)
Subjects: LCSH: Italian Americans—History—Juvenile literature. | Immigrants—United States—History—Juvenile literature. | Italian Americans—Juvenile literature. | Italy—Emigration and immigration—Juvenile literature. | United States—Emigration and immigration—History—Juvenile literature.
Classification: LCC E184.I8 L33 2019 | DDC 973'.00451–dc23

Manufactured in the United States of America

On the cover: Italian Americans parade down Mulberry Street, through the heart of New York City's Little Italy, to celebrate the Feast of San Gennaro, an annual festival honoring the patron saint of Naples and saluting Italian heritage.

CONTENTS

Introduction

Victor Emmanuel II was the last king of Sardinia and the first king of Italy when the country became unified in 1861.

While there had been a small number of Italians living in America dating back to the 1700s, mass immigration to the United States from Italy didn't begin until the late 1800s. More specifically, the history of mass immigration of Italians to America began in 1861. It is marked by three major waves of emigration from Italy.

The first great wave of Italians immigrating to the United States began in 1861 and coincided with the unification of Italy. At that time, various city-states, kingdoms, and provinces united to become the Kingdom of Italy. Before 1860, the peninsula of Italy was divided into kingdoms ruled by nobility, providences controlled by neighboring countries, the Papal States managed by the Roman Catholic Church, and privately owned estates. The unification of the Kingdom of Italy was meant to unite these groups, but it led to widespread poverty, higher taxes, and higher unemployment. Italy's strict class system negatively impacted Italians and left peasants and farmers with few opportunities to improve their lives. These harsh and restrictive conditions motivated the first major wave of Italians to leave the country in search of better opportunities.

Italians who arrived in America immediately sought out jobs and homes. Some Italian immigrants intended to stay long enough to make some money and then return home. But most ended up staying in America and sending for their loved ones once they had housing and stable jobs.

Italians found English and American customs difficult to learn, and some Americans harbored anti-immigration attitudes. But Italian immigrants persisted in creating communities and adapting to American life.

The second wave began in 1900 and ended at the start of World War I. The third wave began after World War II and ended in 1976. While many Italians supported both war efforts and enlisted in the US military, anti-immigration attitudes rose to hostile levels. There were stretches of time when Italians were turned away for jobs, forced to register as enemy aliens, and looked upon with deep suspicion.

As America settled into postwar life, the American economy boomed and life for Italians changed. Many Italians moved out of their ethnic enclaves in urban areas and into the suburbs, where they assimilated more fully into American life. They contributed significantly to American culture, politics, sports, and entertainment. As new generations of children of Italian families were born on American soil, Italian American families began to flourish and grow. Many purchased homes, earned college degrees, and launched businesses. By the end of the twentieth century, Italian immigrants became one of the largest groups of Europeans to resettle in America.

For an immigrant group that fled horrible living conditions at home only to find difficult conditions in the United States, Italian Americans found a way to persevere and to become a significant influence on American culture and society.

VISA   UNITED STATE

Life in Italy

The first settlements of Rome, Italy's capital, date back to 753 BCE. The land has been a crossroads for major moments in world history, from the fall of the Roman Empire to the birth of the Renaissance. Venice, a city of waterways and canals, and Milan, the country's fashion capital, are full of influential architecture, culture, museums, textiles, and cuisine. But modern Italy is quite different from the country of 1861, when the land and its people were divided and disjointed.

THE LAND OF ITALY

Italy lies on a peninsula located in southern Europe. Modern Italy has an area of 116,346 square miles (301,335 square kilometers) and shares open borders with the nations of France, Austria, Switzerland and Slovenia.

Italy's most recognizable geographic feature is the country's bootlike shape. The country consists of the mainland as well as several islands, including Sicily and Sardinia. The Alps, the highest and most extensive mountain range in Europe, are spread among eight European nations, including Italy, in the northern part of the country. Running down the center of the country are the Apennine Mountains. Because the country is a massive peninsula that juts out into the Mediterranean Sea, Italy has more than 4,700 miles (7,564 kilometers) of coastline. The Mediterranean Sea lies to the south and east. The Tyrrhenian Sea, which is part of the Mediterranean Sea, is along the western coast of Italy.

The mountains of Italy are very cold and wet, and they receive snow and ice in the winter months. In the southern coastal areas, it is often rainy in the winters and hot, humid, and dry in the summers.

A DIVIDED COUNTRY

Prior to 1815, the Italian peninsula was a collection of decidedly separate kingdoms, city-states, Papal States, and duchies. Roughly twenty-five million people lived in these various regions of the country. The main entities were the Kingdom

These maps show Italy as it was in 1862, with northern Italy on top and southern Italy on the bottom.

of Sardinia, the Kingdom of the Two Sicilies, and the Papal States. Each entity had its own government, cultural traditions, and foods.

There were also different dialects of the Italian language. Because of the many regions of Italy, the country lacked a single national language. Toscano, which became the modern-day language of Italian, was used only as a literary language and was spoken by people who lived in the region of Tuscany. Elsewhere, many different dialects of Toscano were spoken. Piedmontese was a version of the Italian language spoken by those living in Piedmont, a region in northwest Italy.

The Roman Catholic Church was based in Italy, and the vast majority of people practiced Catholicism. The Papal States were territories located in central Italy, and they were ruled over by the pope, who was the head of the church.

Italy's political environment was unstable. The Papal States were located in the center of the country and divided the Italian peninsula in two. This division left Italy with a northern region and a southern region. Austria and France each dominated different northern Italian provinces, while duchies and private estates made up most of the southern region. Conflict and invasions of neighboring peoples caused violence and upheaval.

Italy had a rigid class structure during this time period. There were two main classes in society before the Italian unification: the aristocracy, or the noble class, and the peasants. The aristocracy consisted of kings and other wealthy individuals who received their titles, wealth, and land through right of birth. The peasants were poor, working-class people who were often

VISA UNITED STATES

Giovanni Maria Mastai Ferretti, also known as Pope Pius IX, ruled the Roman Catholic Church in Italy from 1846 until 1878.

skilled in a craft, such as metalwork, masonry, or carpentry, or they worked the land as farmers. There was no opportunity to move among the classes, which meant if you were born into a peasant family, you could expect to remain a peasant for life.

THE RISORGIMENTO ADVANCES

As the population grew and became more involved in government, a collective interest in unifying the country into one nation grew into more than just desire. There was a middle class that began to take shape as the country began to unify. These people worked in jobs that supported the nobility, such as lawyers, accountants, and traders. However, the class structure was still very rigid and provided opportunity for very little mobility.

Meanwhile, a period of difficult political and social struggle ensued between 1815 and 1871. All of the separate regions, Papal States, city-states, and estates unified into the Kingdom of Italy on March 17, 1861, under the rule of King Victor Emmanuel II.

After the Risorgimento of 1861, Italy began to modernize. The new nation adopted a democratic constitution, and industrialization began, with factories in the north, which had been the center of trade since the Renaissance. Wealth was concentrated in the north, and even though the country was unified, there was little interest in spreading wealth beyond the northern part of the country.

ECONOMIC INEQUALITY

The south remained largely agricultural. Many of these farms were owned by wealthy Italians who lived in the north. As the northern cities flourished, the south remained very poor and gained very little economic benefit from the unification. The north refused to share its resources with the southern half of the country. In addition, the population in all of Europe was growing, and jobs were becoming more and more difficult to find in Italy and elsewhere.

In the south, Italians faced horrible poverty, malnutrition, a weak economy, and poor living conditions. In many southern townships and villages, water was a luxury and roads were nearly impassible during the harsh winter months. The economy in the south struggled as taxes increased on farmers and skilled workers failed to find work.

A few wealthy families who lived in the north owned most of the land in the south, but they failed to make sure the land was cared for properly. Instead of being directly involved in managing the land, the northern landowners allowed others to oversee their properties and to run their southern estates. This led to a number of problems for farmers. The land was not irrigated, so farmers had a hard time growing crops. And trees and high shrubs were not planted to help reduce or stop erosion, so formerly usable land gradually became unusable. Farmers not being able to produce anything from the farmland and skilled workers not being able to find jobs led to one thing—rampant poverty.

ITALIAN FARMING AND CROPS

Southern Italian farmers made their living off the land. The long, dry summers of southern Italy were well suited for certain crops, such as olives, which thrived in the heat and dry weather conditions.

Italy's most popular crops during the late 1870s included wheat, tomatoes, olives, grapes, citrus fruits, and a variety of nuts. Hard wheat, used mostly for making pasta, which remains a cornerstone of Italian cuisine, grew predominantly in the south. Tomatoes, the main ingredient in sauces and many Italian dishes, were shipped throughout the country and were even exported as part of Italy's trading of goods. The taste and quality of olive oil was enhanced by the long, dry summers. Nearly all regions of Italy grew grapes and produced wine. However, the hot, arid southern region helped to cultivate very sweet grapes that were used to produce sweeter, heavier wines such as marsala. These wines were popular for use in cooking, not as a beverage. Citrus fruits, such as lemons and tangerines, were popular crops in Italy. Sicily and Puglia, two southern regions of the country, were known for their hazelnut and almond crops.

Disease also took its toll on southern Italians. The south endured outbreaks of cholera and malaria, and a mysterious parasite began to destroy many of the grapevines in the region.

Following the Risorgimento, southern Italians faced many hardships, including widespread poverty and outbreaks of disease. In this engraving, government officials visit a hospital in Naples during a cholera epidemic.

Thousands of Italians found themselves in worsening living conditions and with little means to support themselves and their families.

Italians began to seek out a new place to live. The unification also freed Italians to move around to different parts of the country or leave the nation altogether. As a result, Italians saw immigrating to the United States as an opportunity to break free of the limitations of their social class and to achieve greater economic success. They began to immigrate to the United States to try to find work and to improve their lives.

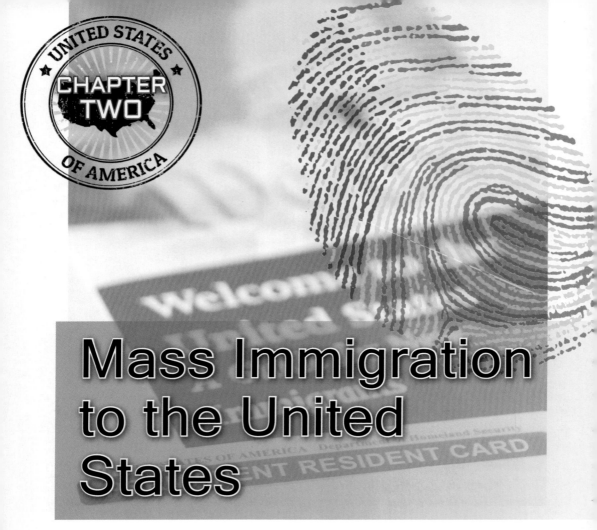

Mass Immigration to the United States

The first wave of immigrants consisted mostly of northern Italians who made their livings as shopkeepers and artisans. They were middle-class peasants who saw America as a new place to sell their goods and services. These Italians had a little bit of money, but Italy's class system would discount their wealth because they lacked royal relations.

As Italians left Italy, they immigrated to a number of countries that provided better opportunities than what they had left behind. Many Italian immigrants chose to start new lives

VISA
UNITED STATES
OF AMERICA

This photograph from the late 1800s shows working-class people on a street in the northern Italian city of San Remo. Such shopkeepers and artisans were among the first to leave Italy to seek a better life.

in Brazil, Argentina, Canada, and to a lesser extent, Australia and Africa.

And then, there were those who came to the United States. Between 1861 and 1870, twenty-five thousand Italians left Italy for the United States. But Italian immigrants would soon learn that creating a better life in the United States would not be easy.

DIFFICULT PASSAGE

Passage on the steamships traveling across the Atlantic Ocean at the time was not comfortable, enjoyable, or even safe. If this migration via transatlantic travel had occurred in the early 1830s, the trip would have taken forty days. By the 1880s, steamship technology had advanced such that the trip required just a week. Still, ships were overcrowded. Immigrants were often held in third-class steerage, in dark, cramped quarters below the deck. They were not allowed on deck.

The journey was also highly unsanitary. Most third-class travelers slept in their clothes for the entire journey. They had limited bathing amenities and were not able to take baths for the duration of the trip. They were fed stews or soups with a piece of bread, and illness was common in the cramped, unmaintained living spaces.

One of the few positives of this experience was that it served to unify Italian immigrants, who were coming from different parts of Italy. The unification of Italy was supposed to create a common Italian state, where all Italians were now part of one country and one ethnic group. But they lacked a common shared history or experience. For those who left, their travel experience provided that first feeling of solidarity with other Italians.

ELLIS ISLAND: THE GATEWAY TO AMERICA

The Italians who chose the United States as their new home arrived through the Ellis Island Immigration Center in New York. When immigrants arrived on Ellis Island, they found

As immigrants arrived in America, they came through Ellis Island. For more than sixty years, Ellis Island was the nation's busiest immigrant inspection station.

themselves shuffled into a strange, chaotic, and confusing experience that served to process and document their arrival. Immigrants were sorted and underwent a series of inspections, during which immigration agents checked for physical fitness and mental stability.

As immigrants arrived, families were separated. Men were herded into one area, and women and children were brought to another. Immigration officials conducted a medical inspection to screen for deformities or health problems. If an immigrant had a medical condition, their clothing was marked in white chalk with an abbreviation for the ailment. *H* meant heart problems, *Pg* meant pregnancy, and *E* meant eye problems. If the medical condition was severe enough, such as a deformity or mental illness, or if an immigrant was deemed too frail for manual labor, the immigrant was sent back to their home country. Others might be held in special housing until they could be cured of their ailment. While only 2 percent of Italians were turned back to Italy after failing their processing inspection, Ellis Island became known to Italians as L'Isola dell Lagrime, or the Island of Tears.

Once cleared by the physical and mental examinations, immigrants were then required to answer a number of questions, such as: What is your name and age?; Are you married or single?; Do you have an occupation or skill?; Can you read and write?; What is your nationality?; and Where in the United States are you going?

Immigration officials asked the separated men and women the same questions to see if their answers were the same. If answers were contradictory, further questioning was conducted.

LIKE HOME: ROSETO, PENNSYLVANIA

In 1882, among the first to leave Italy was a group of Italian men from the village of Roseto Valfortore. They left Italy to escape oppressive poverty and found their way to Pennsylvania. They settled a small village in the foothills of the Pocono Mountains. They named the new town Roseto, after their Italian village.

Roseto, Pennsylvania, became an ethnic enclave, or community, that mirrored life in Roseto Valfortore. Roseto's residents spoke the same regional Italian dialect and re-created their village, down to a replica of its design, in their new village. Many of the men in Roseto worked in the neighboring towns on the railroad or in the local quarries. As they made more money, they sent for family members. Consequently, the town grew into a self-contained community, with its own bakery and farms. The community members supported one another as they preserved their Italian heritage and customs.

The entire processing experience could take anywhere from three to six hours.

A NEW HOME

As immigrants from around the world were granted access to the United States after passing through Ellis Island, many saw New York City as a way station, or a temporary stop. This was not the experience of Italians. More than one-third of all Italian immigrants who arrived in the United States stayed in one of New York City's boroughs, or they moved on to towns and cities in New Jersey.

Those who settled in Lower Manhattan established a neighborhood around Mulberry Street, known as Little Italy. Others traveled beyond New York to find work in other major cities, such as Boston, Philadelphia, Chicago, San Francisco, Baltimore, and New Orleans. These cities also established

Mulberry Street, the main thoroughfare through New York City's Little Italy, was the center of activity for an enclave that welcomed thousands of Italian immigrants.

ethnic neighborhood enclaves, similar to Little Italy. These enclaves provided a community of people with the same values and traditions.

Many Italian immigrants began working and sending money back to Italy. In many cases, it took several years of working to save up enough to pay the ship passages for family members to leave Italy and join their loved ones in the United States. It was typical for husbands to leave Italy and send money for their wives and children to join them later.

Americans began to treat Italians poorly as soon as the first wave of Italian immigrants arrived. Seen as strange and different for their language, customs, and religion, many Americans called Italian immigrants derogatory names that insulted their heritage and ancestry. Many stores refused to sell groceries, housewares, and clothing to Italians. Some landlords refused to rent them apartments. This was not a situation that would be fixed overnight.

New Immigration

By 1900, conditions worsened in Italy. This caused a second wave of Italian immigration at the turn of the century. During this wave, roughly nine million Italians arrived in the United States between 1900 and 1914. This wave was the beginning of a new era of immigration in the United States.

VISA
UNITED STATES OF AMERIC

CHANGING DEMOGRAPHICS

This new era of immigration marked a major change from prior demographic trends of immigration, sometimes referred to as old immigration, which consisted of Germans, Irish, British, and Scandinavians immigrating to the United States between 1820 and 1880. People from Scotland, Holland, and France also came. These groups shared the same attitudes and similar ethnic, cultural, and religious backgrounds as those who helped settle and establish the United States. This connection meant that the ideas, culture, traditions, and attitudes that they shared shaped American society. In addition, the dominant religion of the United States at this time was the Protestant faith, which, unlike the Roman Catholic religion, had no hierarchy of leadership inside its church organization.

The new wave of immigration to the United States included Italians along with Slavs, Jews, Japanese, Poles, Serbians, Croatians, Chinese, and Russians. They arrived between 1880 and 1930. This was a group of immigrants who had little to no historical connection to the United States or to anyone living there. And many had physical characteristics like darker skin tones and non-Anglo facial features and hair colors that easily identified them as being part of the new wave of immigration. Further, many practiced non-Christian religions like Judaism, Taoism, Buddhism, and Shinto that were unfamiliar to most Americans. Many Italians, in particular, were Catholic. The Roman Catholic Church was led by the pope, and this led some Americans to fear that the pope, as a result of the growing number of Roman Catholic immigrants in America, would end up ruling the country.

Another thing that made those descended from the earlier generations of immigration uncomfortable was the different clothing, hairstyles, and cultures of the new immigrants. The differences between these two groups bred a sense of separation and alienation between the old and the new.

While all regions of Italy were represented, the largest number of Italian immigrants came from Mezzogiorno, or southern Italy. They represented such regions as Calabria, Campania, Abruzzi, Molise, and Sicily. The majority of these immigrants were farm laborers, or *contadini*. A small population were craftsmen, including those skilled as carpenters, bricklayers, masons, tailors, and barbers. Those who left, the vast majority of whom were men, left Italy with little or no money but with skills they hoped to use to make a living once they had settled in their new adopted countries. These peasants made their living as blacksmiths, butchers, fishermen, stonemasons, and miners.

BUILDING COMMUNITIES

As the first Italian immigrants landed on America's shores, finding new places to live and means of support became the first crucial task for survival. But they didn't know the language or understand the country's customs.

Italian immigrants in the United States decided to stick together. They spoke to each other in their own language and sought to protect one another. In many major cities,

Italian immigrants settled together in neighborhoods. These neighborhoods, like Little Italy in Manhattan, became a way for Italian immigrants to hold on to their culture, food, and rituals.

Living among others who shared the cultural and family traditions of their homeland became a soothing way of life for Italian immigrants. Multigenerational families lived together, and other Italians who spoke their language surrounded them.

However, many Italians found that while living in these neighborhoods helped to preserve the Italian way of life they knew and enjoyed, it led to isolation from American society. By living together, Italian immigrants failed to assimilate into American culture. Many did not learn English.

THE PADRONE SYSTEM

As Italians arrived in the United States, they needed to find work fast. Between around 1880 and 1910, many Italian immigrants became involved with a padrone, or an employment agent who arranged work on behalf of Italian immigrants. *Padrone* is an Italian word that means boss or manager. Many padrones were Italian immigrants who came to America and had become established. The padrone work system was a complex network of business relationships in which padrones would negotiate job opportunities with contractors, shipping companies, quarries and mines, and the railroads.

The padrone would assess a laborer's skills and provide that person with a job. The benefit for Italian immigrants was that they could find work almost immediately upon arriving in

A padrone often stood watch over the immigrants he helped to find jobs, both as a way to control them and to make sure they were efficient and productive.

the United States. Some even wrote letters to padrones before they came to America to let them know they were arriving and would need work. Those people made arrangements with a padrone in advance because of the fear of moving to and living in a large, unfamiliar city. A padrone often escorted immigrant workers to the worksite, ensuring a degree of safety in strange surroundings. Padrones would also help immigrants send money back to Italy to support the immigrant's family.

The disadvantage was that many padrones exploited and practically enslaved their own countrymen. The padrone

VISA UNITED STATE OF AMERIC

often exerted an unfair amount of control over his laborers. Many immigrants didn't know their true wages or how much the padrone took out of their pay for commission. Dishonest padrones with an especially high commission rate sometimes took up to 60 percent of an immigrant's pay.

SARAH WOOL MOORE

Sarah Wool Moore was an American art teacher who taught in Nebraska and New York City from 1875 to 1884. She traveled extensively through Europe to enhance her knowledge of art, including spending a considerable amount of time in Italy learning about Italian art and architecture.

When she returned to New York City in 1900, she founded the Society for the Protection of Italian Immigrants, also called the Society for Italian Immigrants. The group was originally created to help Italian immigrants assimilate to America and assist them in understanding American culture and customs. Moore soon realized that padrones and other labor bosses were taking advantage of many Italian immigrants.

Later that year, Moore and members of her group offered lists of boarding houses with honest

(continued on the next page)

(continued from the previous page)

owners to those arriving in the United States. At the port, the group would meet up with immigrants' ships and help immigrants avoid padrones and other con men who wanted to take advantage of unknowing immigrants. Moore's group offered to

help immigrants find jobs that were beneficial to the immigrant and that did not include commissions to a padrone.

Moore also realized that without adequate language skills, Italian immigrants would not be able to negotiate or fend for themselves. Throughout her involvement with the Society for the

Through the Society for the Protection of Italian Immigrants, Sarah Wool Moore helped Italian immigrants adjust to life in America.

Protection of Italian Immigrants, Moore fought to establish schools where immigrants could quickly learn English and better understand American culture. In 1902, to help Italian immigrants learn English and better assimilate into American society, Moore published an English language guide that contained common English phrases and sentences that Italians would need to know to help communicate at work and in their daily lives.

In industry, trade unions that fought for livable wages and shorter work hours did not include Italians. The unions were scared that Italian immigrants would be willing to work for any amount of money. Padrones who were eager to fulfill contracts might have offered work at low rates that unions didn't approve of, so padrones may have contributed to trade unions neglecting or resenting Italian immigrants. Members of trade unions also had fears that Italians would completely replace American workers. Such trade unions sometimes preferred to pick fights with other workers instead of with employers as a means of advancing their goals.

Several factors contributed to the decline of the padrone system. The federal government enacted a number of immigration policies to either limit immigration or tax the arrival of immigrants into the United States. This limited the supply of incoming laborers who could benefit padrones. The padrone system also began to decline as Italians became more

Samuel Gompers was the first and longest-serving president of the American Federation of Labor. He was influential in establishing the American labor movement.

VISA UNITED STATE

self-sufficient and less reliant on padrones. As immigrants learned English and learned how to negotiate jobs and wages for themselves, even legitimate padrones became less and less useful to laborers.

As Italian immigrants worked to settle in the United States and establish new lives, circumstances were brewing in Europe that would lead to the outbreak of World War I in 1914.

After World War I

I talians looked different, ate different foods, spoke an unfamiliar language, settled together in separate neighborhoods, and isolated themselves from American life. It wasn't their fault that people who came from all over the world to the United States weren't as homogenous as Americans wanted them to be, but these differences were the basis of why Americans were unwilling to trust them or treat them well. This environment became law as the United States began to rely on

VISA

quotas. However, the Italian American community found some success in the period between World War I and the late 1920s.

WORLD WAR I: TAKING SIDES

From 1900 until 1914, major European powers Great Britain, Germany, France, Russia, Austria-Hungary, and Italy struggled to maintain a balance of power amid shifting alliances, strengthening militaries, and growing tensions in the region. However, four factors were building toward an international conflict. The first, militarism, is when countries continually build up their military resources. The second was alliances between countries. No one really knew which side most countries supported in these secretive agreements. The third factor, imperialism, is the competition between European countries to dominate colonies around the world and claim territory from other imperial powers as sources for raw materials or markets for their goods. The fourth factor that contributed to World War I was nationalism, or pride in one's own country. This pride leads to people putting their nation above all others and wanting glory for it. Historically, glory has been earned in a successful campaign of war.

Together, these factors form a memorable acronym: MAIN. It is worth noting that if only one of these factors existed at that time, it wouldn't have had such devastating consequences as a massive, far-reaching war. In other words, World War I was the result of many catastrophic policies that many countries carried out during the same time period.

The spark that started World War I was the assassination of Archduke Franz Ferdinand of Austria on July 28, 1914. Some rebels in the country of Serbia were behind the assassination. Austria-Hungary then declared war on Serbia, and because Serbia had ethnic ties to Russia, Russia declared war on Austria-Hungary. Austria-Hungary had a secret alliance with Germany, so Germany also joined the conflict. The various secret alliances resulted in the Triple Alliance, consisting of Germany, Italy, and Austria-Hungary, and the Triple Entente, consisting of Russia,

The assassination of Austria-Hungary's Archduke Franz Ferdinand (*second from left*) sparked the start of World War I.

France, and Great Britain. The United States later joined the Triple Entente, and Italy later abandoned the Triple Alliance to join the Triple Entente.

Italians living in the United States supported the American war effort by producing goods and enlisting in the US military in large numbers.

POSTWAR PEACE CHANGES ATTITUDES AT HOME

World War I marked the beginning of trench warfare, when technologies such as machine guns, tanks, and hand grenades enabled more violent forms of fighting. At the end of the war, American soldiers returned home and shared stories of their horrific experience. Americans began to look at Europe as a set of nations that were always engaged in some conflict. Those Americans began to wonder why they were entrenched in conflicts happening across the world that had little impact on life at home. This self-reflection led to American isolationist and nativist attitudes. Italian immigrants were caught in the crossfire of these attitudes when the war ended.

This shift in US opinion led the government to enact the Emergency Quota Act of 1921 and the Immigration Act of 1924. These acts put restrictions on the number of immigrants who could be admitted into the United States. The restriction for the Emergency Quota Act of 1921 created the National Origins Formula. This formula limited immigration to 3 percent of the current number of people from any given ethnic group

At the end of World War I, President Woodrow Wilson drew America into a period of isolationism. Attitudes shifted, and immigrants came to be seen as a threat to American life.

VISA   UNITED STATE

living in the United States, based on the 1910 census data. This meant that if the 1910 census counted one thousand British people and one hundred Italians in the United States at the time, after passage of the law, thirty British people could immigrate to the United States each year, while only three Italians could. This example is more or less how the quota played out. A greater number of people coming from northern European countries, whose people were already in the United States in large numbers, were allowed to immigrate, compared to the new immigrant nationals.

The quota became even narrower when the Immigration Act of 1924 adjusted it. After this law was passed, only 2 percent of a given ethnic group's number could enter the United States. That figure was calculated from the 1890 census, a census that counted even fewer immigrants from Italy and the eastern European nations than the 1910 census.

THE RISE OF PREJUDICE AND ANTI-CATHOLIC SENTIMENT

As Americans turned inward and disassociated themselves from all foreign influence, language and attitudes continued to change in the 1920s. Even the names of foods were Americanized. Frankfurters, a sausage that originated in the German city of Frankfurt, were now called hot dogs. This Americanization turned its attention to immigrants.

America was mostly Protestant, and many Protestant Americans looked down on people who subscribed to other religions. Anti-Catholic sentiment grew, and Americans viewed predominantly Catholic immigrant groups, such as Italians, Irish, and others, with suspicion. As more and more immigrants entered the United States, and as the numbers of those practicing Catholicism grew, the American Protestant population became distressed. Americans wondered who Catholics would be loyal to if the president of the United States and the pope, the head of the Catholic Church, disagreed on issues. They also feared that the pope had an interest in taking over the United States.

ITALIAN AMERICANS IMPACT AMERICAN CULTURE

The years between World War I and World War II were a time of growth for Italians in politics, music, film, sports, and more. One significant Italian of the time was Rudolph Valentino.

Rudolph Valentino starred in more than forty films during the silent-film era. He was born Rodolfo Guglielmi in Castellaneta, Italy, on May 6, 1895. He immigrated to the United States in 1913 and soon found work as an actor in romantic dramas in Hollywood. He is widely recognized as Hollywood's first sex symbol, but he wasn't particularly well liked in real life. He died unexpectedly in 1926, at the age of thirty-one.

VISA

UNITED STATES

The growth of the Mafia and organized crime also fueled anti-Italian sentiment. The Mafia was an organized crime organization that originated in Italy and later spread to the United States and other countries. Because Italian American Mafia members like Al Capone and Lucky Luciano became infamous for violence and criminal behavior, many Americans began to fear Italians. Many assumed that most Italians were associated with the Mafia.

POSTWAR LIFE BECOMES MORE PROSPEROUS

The Roaring Twenties became a period of prosperity for America. Even though anti-immigration and anti-Italian attitudes persisted, that era saw Italian American wealth increase. More Italians owned homes. Italians were getting hired as plumbers and carpenters, and other professions were becoming more willing to hire immigrants. Italians were also getting jobs as policemen, firemen, and civil servants. Italian women benefited from more independence in America, and some worked outside the home as secretaries, dressmakers, and in other careers.

As the next generation of Italian American children was born, families took advantage of public schools. Their children learned English, engaged in the sciences, and acquired an education that better prepared them for adult life. This generation of children was also more fully integrated into

As the Roaring Twenties began, immigrants prospered amid tensions in America. Immigrant children went to school, some immigrants owned businesses, and some became American citizens.

American society. They attended school with children from all types of families, and they were more fully immersed in American culture. This also marked the beginning of many Italian families giving their children English names instead of traditional Italian names. Instead of Paulo, a boy would be named Paul, Anthony instead of Antonio, Samuel instead of Salvatore, Mary instead of Maria, for example. It was as if to say that Italians now knew that they belonged.

The Next Global Conflict

As the Roaring Twenties came to a close, two major factors impacted Italian immigration to the United States. The rise of Fascism in Italy led to a mass exodus of Italians seeking a better life and more freedom, and the outbreak of World War II would place strict limits on nearly all immigration.

THE RISE OF FASCISM LEADS TO ITALIAN MIGRATION

Fascism contributed to an intermediary period of Italians immigrating to America. Benito Mussolini, a World War I

Italian fascist dictator Benito Mussolini was a key figure in the tensions in Europe leading up to World War II.

VISA UNITED STATES

veteran and the publisher of numerous socialist newspapers in Italy, established a party called Fasci di Combattimento in 1919. The Fascist Party was a violent organization that engaged in silencing activities against opposing political parties in Italy. Fascism was an ideology or belief system that included intense nationalism, contempt for democratic principles, a social hierarchy that favored the wealthy and elite, and increased control over the people under Fascist rule.

Fascists targeted poor, uneducated Italians. The violence the Fascist Party used to exert control over the Italian people made life unbearable for many. Many Italians fled Italy to escape the Fascist regime that was forming.

By 1922, Mussolini became prime minister of Italy. He ruled the nation as a dictatorship under his own authoritarian control.

THE NEXT WORLDWIDE WAR

In October 1929, after a period of prosperity and growth, the stock market crashed. The United States, as well as other nations around the world, plunged into the Great Depression. Industrial production dropped sharply. This sudden stalling of the economy led to mass layoffs and workers losing their sources of income. Many Americans, including Italian Americans, also lost their homes. As incomes plummeted, families began to suffer from malnourishment and starvation.

The Great Depression lasted until the beginning of World War II, when military needs led to the increased production of services, food, and various goods to support the war effort.

On the morning of December 7, 1941, Japan bombed Naval Station Pearl Harbor, a US naval base. This prompted the United States to enter World War II, which had begun in 1939, against Japan, Germany, and Italy, also known as the Axis powers.

As Americans dealt with the shock of being attacked at home and their country's entry into the war, ethnic Italians, ethnic Germans, and ethnic Japanese people found themselves in a strange position. They were living in a country that had declared war on their homeland.

NEW SUSPICIONS

Within days of the United States declaring war on Italy, Americans began to see Italian Americans as a different kind of threat. Because Mussolini sided with Adolf Hitler and the Axis powers in the war, Americans suddenly felt that there was no way to determine the loyalty of many Italian Americans. Fear set in that Italian immigrants were dangerous or were providing information to the Italian government.

On February 19, 1942, President Franklin Roosevelt signed Executive Order 9066. Originally, the order called for the evacuation of more than 120,000 Japanese Americans from their homes on the West Coast. The order also called for the relocation of more than 10,000 Italian Americans, and it highly restricted the movements of more than 600,000 Italian Americans nationwide. Executive Order 9066 allowed the government to define immigrants as "enemy aliens." It also empowered local law enforcement to arrest and imprison enemy aliens without charges and without a

VISA

trial. The government could also seize homes, businesses, and other property.

Life for many Italian Americans immediately changed. There were many arrests, and agents from the Federal Bureau of Investigation (FBI) and the Office of Strategic Services (which later became the Central Intelligence Agency) made random surveillance visits to neighborhoods known to be predominately Italian. Italian Americans could not speak about the war publicly without fear of arrest, being detained, or being deported, and the US government confiscated short-wave radios that Italian Americans owned. A new nightly curfew

Soon after the United States' entry into World War II, an FBI agent (*left*) escorts a group of Italian and German Americans to Ellis Island for deportation. Many Italian Americans feared being detained or deported.

restricted Italian Americans from leaving their homes between the hours of 8 p.m. and 6 a.m.

In addition, Italian Americans and many other immigrant groups were now required to carry identification on them at all times. The Alien Registration Act of 1940 required that all people living in the United States who were not citizens or nationals register with the government. This registration, which was involuntary, enabled the US government to track immigrants who promoted non-American ideas. The act made it possible for the United States to detain individuals, deny them US citizenship, or deport them back to their home country. The registration process required immigrants to complete a questionnaire and have their fingerprints taken. As many as six hundred thousand Italians living in the United States who had not yet become citizens were now required to carry identity cards identifying them as resident aliens.

AN ITALIAN AMERICAN LEGEND: JOE DIMAGGIO

Joe DiMaggio was born Giuseppe Paolo DiMaggio on November 25, 1914, to Guiseppe and Rosalie DiMaggio. His parents were Italian immigrants who came to America in 1898. DiMaggio began playing professional baseball with the San Francisco Seals, a minor league team, as a center fielder in 1932. He drew the attention of the New York Yankees, and

VISA UNITED STATES

that team signed DiMaggio to a multiyear contract. He made his debut for the Yankees on May 3, 1936.

DiMaggio became a legendary baseball player. He set a Yankees record in 1936 by hitting twenty-nine home runs in his rookie season. That record stood until July 2017, when Yankee rookie Aaron Judge broke it. Over the course of his career, he played 1,736 games, he had 2,214 hits, including 361 home runs, and he had 1,390 runs. He played in ten World Series and won nine, and he played in eleven All-Star Games. He was named the American League Most Valuable Player three times in his career with the Yankees. He retired from the Yankees in 1951, and in 1955, he was inducted into the Baseball Hall of Fame.

Joe DiMaggio, whose parents emigrated from Italy, played baseball for the New York Yankees and became a legend for his athletic abilities. He is shown here with his mother, Rosalie.

Even famous Italian Americans and their families were not spared registration. Giuseppe and Rosalie DiMaggio, the parents of legendary baseball player Joe DiMaggio, who was playing for the New York Yankees at the time, were among the thousands of Italian immigrants forced to register as enemy aliens and carry identification. Giuseppe, a fisherman in San Francisco, was barred from fishing in San Francisco Bay, and his fishing boat was seized. This prevented him from earning a living. He was also restricted to traveling within 5 miles (8 kilometers) of his home. He needed a permit to travel beyond that area.

ROSIE THE RIVETER

World War II became a pivotal moment in history for women. They took positions in the military and filled the jobs of men who were enlisted to fight. Women also worked in factories and held position in government organizations.

Rose Bonavita, the daughter of Italian immigrants, was one of the millions of American women who worked in the war industries. Bonavita served as an aircraft riveter during the war. President Roosevelt recognized her work performance in 1943 when he sent her a commendation letter honoring her wartime contributions.

(continued on the next page)

VISA UNITED STATE

During World War II, many women helped the war effort by taking jobs that had traditionally been filled by men.

(continued from the previous page)

She is among a group of women who likely served as the inspiration behind Rosie the Riveter, a character depicted by artist J. Howard Miller for a 1942 poster aimed at recruiting female workers for the munitions industry. The poster, one of the most iconic images of working women during the war, shows a woman flexing her bicep beneath the words "We Can Do It!" A recent article in *Rhetoric & Public Affairs* suggests that the real model for the photo may have been Naomi Parker. Regardless, Bonavita's contribution to the war effort was significant.

ITALIANS REMAIN STRONG

Eager to show that they were not enemies of the United States and to prove their love for their adopted homeland, many Italian American men enlisted in the US military to fight in the war effort. Italians ended up enlisting in World War II at a higher rate than any other immigrant group in the United States.

One notably successful ethnic Italian American who fought in World War II was Colonel Henry Mucci, who served in the US Army Rangers. He led one of the most successful rescue missions in US history by leading his force to free 511 survivors of the Bataan Death March from a Japanese prison camp in the Philippines.

Enrico Fermi, an Italian immigrant, was an important physicist who helped in the creation of the first atomic bomb.

Another ethnic Italian who contributed to the US war effort was Enrico Fermi. Fermi was born in Rome, Italy, in 1901 and immigrated to the United States in 1938 after becoming a nuclear physicist. He became one of the leading physicists on the Manhattan Project, which developed nuclear energy and the first atomic bomb. Fermi was awarded the Nobel Prize in Physics for discovering new elements, but it eventually became clear that what he had discovered were modified elements that were the product of fission.

VISA UNITED STAT

Postwar Life for Italian Americans

The end of the war marked a change in attitude toward Italian immigrants in the United States. The vast majority of Italian immigrants supported the United States in the war effort by serving in the military and by working in jobs that supplied goods to the war front. This show of loyalty caused negative attitudes about Italian immigrants to dissipate.

And then, a third wave of Italian immigration to the United States began. After six years of war, many Italians dreamed of a fresh start.

MANGIA! ITALIAN CUISINE IN AMERICA

One of the most significant contributions of Italians to American life was the infusion of Italian cuisine. Italian pasta dishes, meatballs, sausage, and a variety of cheeses and desserts all led to Italian cuisine becoming one of the most popular ethnic foods in America.

Italian cuisine in the United States dates back to the start of mass immigration in the 1900s. As Italian neighborhoods began to spring up in cities around the country, cuisine was a way for Italians

Little Italy in New York City, with its many Italian restaurants, remains a haven for Italian culture.

VISA UNITED STAT

to maintain their cultural traditions and family ties to their homeland. Italians opened restaurants and Italian markets. These places helped to bring Italian delicacies to the masses. Soon, Italian foods and specialty items could be found around the country.

THE CHANGING FACE OF IMMIGRATION

The US government relied on the National Origins Formula until 1965, when the Immigration and Nationality Act of 1965 replaced it. This new system of vetting immigrants was based on an immigrant's skill level as well as on family relationships with current US citizens or residents. Following the end of the National Origins Formula, the United States saw an increase in immigration from Italy and other European countries. But the face of immigration was changing. The United States was now welcoming immigrants from a diverse range of countries, including China, India, Mexico, Canada, Cuba, the Dominican Republic, and El Salvador.

Based on the 2000 census, more than fifteen million people self-identified as Italian American. As of the 2000 census, Italian Americans became the nation's fourth-largest group with European ancestry. The only three European ancestry groups with more people identifying themselves as such were the Germans, the Irish, and the English.

Many of the new immigrants were skilled in various trades or were professionals. Some had an education, and many were able to assimilate immediately.

ACHIEVING THE AMERICAN DREAM

Many Italian Americans moved to the suburbs after World War II. Many went to college to earn degrees. With an education, there were more job opportunities, and these opportunities led Italians to affluence and wealth. In addition, the newer generations of Italian children were more assimilated to American life. In many cases, they identified equally as being Italian and American. This was in contrast to their parents' and grandparents' experiences and attitudes. These new generations also began to marry non-Italians, to the chagrin of traditional members of the previous generations.

As Italian Americans entered the middle class and become more affluent, more and more began to attend college and earn degrees. In the years since the end of World War II, many Italian Americans have begun to rise to leadership positions in American politics and law. Mario Cuomo, the son of Italian immigrants, served as the fifty-second governor of New York for three terms between 1983 and 1994. His son, Andrew Cuomo, later became the fifty-sixth governor of New York.

Representative Nancy Pelosi (D-CA) became the first woman and the first Italian American Speaker of the House of Representatives in 2007. Pelosi was a key figure in passing

VISA UNITED STATE

Mario Cuomo, New York's first Italian American governor, and Nancy Pelosi, the first woman and first Italian American to be Speaker of the House of Representatives, attend a gala for the arts.

the Affordable Care Act (ACA). The ACA brought health care to many Americans who had gone without. Pelosi has been a fierce supporter of environmental conservation and measures to combat climate change.

The story of ethnic Italians in the United States continues to change with each day. The Italian diaspora can now boast

MADE IN HOLLYWOOD: STEREOTYPES ABOUT ITALIANS IN FILM

The portrayal of Italians in film has rarely been balanced. Most storylines featuring Italians portray them as criminals or gangsters connected to organized crime. Movies depicting the close-knit nature of the Italian American family are rare, as are portraits of Italian business owners, politicians, teachers, and community leaders. *The Sopranos* was a critically and commercially successful TV series that centered around an Italian family whose patriarch was the head of a crime organization. Countless movies, such as *The Godfather* and its sequels, have built upon the idea that Italian men are angry and uneducated, and Italian women are overly emotional and overbearing to their children. These stereotypes have served to shape attitudes about Italian Americans for generations.

VISA UNITED STATE

of having connections that didn't exist in the mid-nineteenth century and an impact that is visible in all corners of American society. The greater challenges of the past are now over, but dealing with those challenges has left a somewhat neglected community. Those in the younger generation of Italians have been more inclined to leave their previously insular communities—Roseto, Pennsylvania, for example—to seek opportunities elsewhere. Thus, opportunistic migration for a better life hasn't ended because there is perhaps even greater advancement to gain. This search for better suggests that there are many Italians who aren't completely satisfied with what they have found and achieved thus far. However, ethnic Italians who have settled down are committed to their identity as Americans.

MYTHS AND FACTS

MYTH

All Italian immigrants were in the Mafia.

FACT

While the Mafia originated in Italy and had a significant presence as an organized crime organization in the United States at the turn of the twentieth century, not every Italian was involved in or even knew members of the Mafia. But stories about the Mafia and many of its infamous members helped to create the illusion that Italians were either members or supporters of the crime organization.

MYTH

Italian immigrants wanted the pope to rule the United States.

FACT

While most Italians were Roman Catholic and supported the pope, the pope was not a political leader. Italian Americans supported the US government, followed its laws and social customs, and even enlisted in the military to support the nation as it went to war.

MYTH

Italians talk with their hands.

FACT

Italians often use gestures when speaking to add emphasis to a point or to express more animated feelings about a topic.

VISA

UNITED STATES

ITALIAN AMERICANS

Population in the United States
Approximately 17,000,000 (2016 estimate)

States with the Most Italian Americans
New York: 2,400,328
Pennsylvania: 1,482,538
California: 1,466,083
New Jersey: 1,393,041
Florida: 1,207,516
Massachusetts: 862,392
Illinois: 761,565
Ohio: 737,896
Connecticut: 602,691
Texas: 502,848
(2016 estimates)

Italian Dishes
Pasta
Arancini
Lasagna
Gelato
Tiramisu

Notable Scientists and Inventors
Dr. Enrico Fermi won the 1938 Nobel Prize in Physics before helping to develop the first atomic bomb.

Antonio Meucci developed electromagnetic transmission of vocal sound. His invention led to the invention of the telephone.

Andrew Toti invented the inflatable life jacket.

Notable Entertainers
Sofia Coppola is a prominent Hollywood screenwriter and director. Her films include *Marie Antoinette* and *The Beguiled*.

Lady Gaga, born Stefani Germanotta, is a singer known for her elaborate costumes and theatrical performances.

Frank Sinatra became famous as a singer and movie actor in the 1940s.

Jimmy Kimmel is a comedian and the host of the late-night talk show *Jimmy Kimmel Live!*

Notable Businesses Owned by Italians or Italian Americans
Contadina Food Company
Barnes & Noble
Ghirardelli Chocolate Company
Subway

TIMELINE

1861 The Risorgimento unifies the peninsula of Italy. The first wave of Italian immigration to the United States begins.

1870 The first wave of Italian immigration to the United States ends.

1882 A group of Italian men establish the village of Roseto in Pennsylvania.

1900 The second major wave of Italian immigration begins.

1914 The second wave ends.

1915 Italy joins World War I on the side of the Triple Entente.

1919 Benito Mussolini founds the Fascist Party in Italy.

1921 The Emergency Quota Act of 1921 greatly restricts the number of Italian immigrants who can enter the United States.

1929 The Great Depression plunges the United States into economic despair.

1936 Joe DiMaggio plays his first baseball game with the New York Yankees.

1939 World War II breaks out in Europe. Mussolini sides with Adolf Hitler and the Axis powers.

1940 The Alien Registration Act is enacted and requires many immigrants, including Italians, to register and be fingerprinted, among other things.

1941 After the Japanese bomb Pearl Harbor, the United States enters World War II.

1945 World War II ends and the third wave of Italian immigration begins.

1965 The Immigration and Nationality Act of 1965 lifts the national origins quota and changes immigration requirements.

1975 The third wave of Italian immigration to the United States ends.

1983 Mario Cuomo becomes the first Italian American governor of New York State.

2000 More than fifteen million Italian Americans are living in the United States, according to the US Census Bureau.

2007 Nancy Pelosi becomes the first Italian American Speaker of the US House of Representatives.

VISA

GLOSSARY

agents Representatives who help people in a field that the helped individual is not familiar with.

ancestry The origin or ethnic descent of a person or his or her family.

architecture The art and science of designing buildings and other structures.

cholera An infection of the intestines.

dialect A language or a regional variation within a language that people in a certain region or social group speak.

diaspora A group of people who have been through a large-scale migration from their home country to another location.

duchy A territory, estate, or region of land ruled over by a duke or duchess.

emigrate To leave one's own country and settle in another country.

enclave A small community of cultural or ethnic minorities located within a larger city or territory.

erosion The gradual destruction of land or soil.

hierarchy A system in which people are ranked by status or authority.

immigrate To come to live in a new country.

imperialism A foreign policy that has the goal of asserting power and influence over the people of weaker countries in order to benefit the powerful nation financially.

isolationist A national ideology of turning inward and refusing to get involved in wars and conflicts that involve other countries.

malaria An illness spread by mosquitoes that causes flulike symptoms and death if left untreated.

militarism The building up of one's own military forces.

nationalism A feeling of pride in one's own country; patriotism.

nativist A person or group who assumes that people born elsewhere, such as immigrants, are a threat to the country's economy, safety, or way of life.

production The making of various products and goods.

riveter A person who used a machine to apply rivets to aircraft.

stereotype A common generalization about a racial, ethnic, religious, or other category or group of people.

textiles Material that is suitable for making shirts and other flexible clothing.

Canadian Museum of History
100 Laurier Street
Gatineau, QB K1A 0M8
Canada
Website: http://www.historymuseum.ca
Facebook and Twitter: @CanMusHistory
This museum holds exhibits, collections, and activities for
people interested in Canadian sociology.

Canadian Society for Italian Studies
University of Florida
College of Liberal Arts and Sciences
2014 Turlington Hall
PO Box 117300
Gainesville, FL 32611-7300
(352) 392-2230
Website: http://www.canadiansocietyforitalianstudies.camp7.org
Facebook: @aaiscsis
The Canadian Society for Italian Studies offers presentations
and encourages discussion of research on Italian language,
literature, film, politics and culture, and related fields.

Center for Italian and Italian-American Culture
411 Pompton Avenue, Suite 5
Cedar Grove, NJ 07009
(973) 571-1995
Website: http://www.ciiacofnj.org
Facebook and Twitter: @ciiac
The Center for Italian and Italian-American Culture is

dedicated to promoting, preserving, and celebrating the culture of Italian Americans.

Italian American Museum
155 Mulberry Street
New York, NY 10013
(212) 965-9000
Website: http://www.italianamericanmuseum.org
Facebook: @ItalianAmericanMuseum
Twitter: @iammuseumnyc
The Italian American Museum features memorabilia, documents, exhibitions, and lectures on the Italian American experience.

National Italian American Foundation
Ambassador Peter F. Secchia Building
1860 19th Street NW
Washington, DC 20009
(202) 387-0600
Website: http://www.niaf.org
Facebook and Twitter: @niaf.org
The National Italian American Foundation's mission is to be a resource for the Italian American community and to help preserve Italian American heritage and culture in the United States.

National Organization of Italian American Women
25 West 43rd Street, Suite 1005
New York, NY 10036

(212) 642-2003
Website: http://www.noiaw.org
Facebook: @NOIAW
Twitter: @noiaw
This organization serves to unite and connect women
through Italian culture and heritage and to celebrate the
achievements of women who are of Italian ancestry.

Order Sons of Italy Canada
200-152 Jackson Street East
Hamilton, Ontario L8N 1L3
Canada
(905) 572-7220
Website: http://ordersonsofitalycanada.com
Also known as the Sons of Italy, the organization works to
keep Italian traditions alive and to honor Italian heritage
in Canada.

UNICO National
Fairfield Commons
271 US Highway
46 West, Suite F-103
Fairfield, NJ 07004
(973) 808-0035
Website: http://www.unico.org
Facebook: @uniconational
UNICO is the largest Italian American service organization. It
promotes service to local communities around the world.

Cortopassi, Dino. *Getting Ahead: A Family's Journey from Italian Serfdom to American Success*. Stockton, CA: Black Hole Press, 2014.

Coy, John. *Their Greatest Gift: Courage, Sacrifice, and Hope in a New Land*. Minneapolis, MN: Lerner Publishing Group, 2016.

Cunningham, Anne C. *Critical Perspectives on Immigrants and Refugees* (Analyzing the Issues). New York, NY: Enslow Publishers, 2016.

Eggers, Dave, and Shawn Harris. *Her Right Foot*. San Francisco, CA: Chronicle Books, 2017.

Gagne, Tammy. *The Evolution of Government and Politics in Italy*. Hockessin, DE: Mitchell Lane Publishers, 2015.

Henriquez, Cristina. *The Book of Unknown Americans*. New York, NY: Vintage/Knopf Doubleday, 2015.

Messi, Paolo. *The Real Italy: Your Need-to-Know Guide for All Things Italian*. London, UK: Franklin Watts, 2013.

Roberts, Adrian John. *The Italian Wars*. Auckland, New Zealand: Horsham House, 2014.

Schafer, Steve. *The Border*. Naperville, IL: Sourcebooks, 2017.

Tieck, Sarah. *Italy*. Minneapolis, MN: ABDO Publishing Company, 2014.

BIBLIOGRAPHY

Beck, Roger B., Linda Black, Larry S. Krieger, Phillip C. Naylor, and Dahia Ibo Shabaka. *World History: Patterns of Intersection.* New York, NY: Holt McDougal, 2010.

Cannato, Vincent J. "What Sets Italian Americans Off from Other Immigrants?" National Endowment for the Humanities, January/February 2015. https://www.neh .gov/humanities/2015/januaryfebruary/feature/what-sets -italian-americans-other-immigrants.

Dal Cerro, Bill. "Why No Outrage Over the Offensive Stereotypes on 'Sopranos'?" *Los Angeles Times*, July 26, 1999. http://articles.latimes.com/1999/jul/26 /entertainment/ca-59628.

Dornin, Rusty. "'Secret' of WWII: Italian-Americans Forced to Move." CNN, September 21, 1997. http://www.cnn .com/US/9709/21/italian.relocation.

Hibbert, Christopher. "Benito Mussolini." *Encyclopedia Britannica*, July 18, 2017. https://www.britannica.com /biography/Benito-Mussolini.

History.com staff. "Rosie the Riveter." Retrieved October 17, 2017. http://www.history.com/topics/world-war-ii/rosie -the-riveter.

Lariccia, Ben. "Italian Americans and World War I." *La Gazzetta Italiana*, July 2015. http://www .lagazzettaitaliana.com/history-culture/7891-italian -americans-and-world-war-i.

Library of Congress. "Library of Congress: The Great Arrival." Retrieved October 17, 2017. https://www.loc.gov /teachers/classroommaterials/presentationsandactivities /presentations/immigration/italian3.html.

Mancuso, Janice Therese. "A Brief History of Italian Food in America." *La Gazzetta Italiana*, November 2010. http://www.lagazzettaitaliana.com/food-and-wine/7627-a-brief-history-of-italian-food-in-america.

Molnar, Alexandra. "History of Italian Immigration. (From Europe to America: Immigration Through Family Tales)". Mount Holyoke, December 15, 2010. https://www.mtholyoke.edu/~molna22a/classweb/politics/Italianhistory.html.

Nobelprize.org. "Enrico Fermi–Biography." Retrieved October 16, 2017. https://www.nobelprize.org/nobel_prizes/physics/laureates/1938/fermi-bio.html.

Rapczynski, Joan. "The Italian Immigrant Experience in America (1870–1920)." Yale-New Haven Teachers Institute. Retrieved October 17, 2017. http://teachersinstitute.yale.edu/curriculum/units/1999/3/99.03.06.x.html.

Ricciardelli, Michael. "Research Debunks Identity of 'Rosie the Riveter' in 'We Can Do It!' Poster." Seton Hall University, May 27, 2016. https://www.shu.edu/communication-arts/news/research-debunks-id-of-rosie-the-riveter.cfm.

Statue of Liberty - Ellis Island Foundation, The. "Immigration Timeline." Retrieved October 17, 2017. https://www.libertyellisfoundation.org/immigration-timeline.

Taylor, Alan. "World War II: Women at War." *The Atlantic*, September 11, 2011. https://www.theatlantic.com/photo/2011/09/world-war-ii-women-at-war/100145.

INDEX

ABOUT THE AUTHOR

Laura La Bella's family immigrated to the United States in the early 1900s from Borgo a Mozzano, a town in the province of Lucca, in northern Italy. For generations, they lived in Rome, New York, where her grandparents owned an Italian restaurant called the Cavalier. La Bella lives in Rochester, New York, with her husband and two sons.

PHOTO CREDITS

Cover, p. 3 Pacific Press/LightRocket/Getty Images; p. 6 DEA/A. Dagli Orti/DeAgostini/Getty Images; p. 11 Buyenlarge/Archive Photos/Getty Images; p. 13 DEA Picture Library/DeAgostini /Getty Images; p. 17 Print Collector/Hulton Archive/Getty Images; p. 19 Alinari Archives/Alinari/Getty Images; p. 21 Fotosearch /Archive Photos/Getty Images; pp. 24, 30, 34, 38, 40 Library of Congress Prints and Photographs; p. 32 Nebraska State Historical Society, RG2411 Portraits; p. 44 JHU Sheridan Libraries/Gado /Archive Photos/Getty Images; p. 46 Keystone/Hulton Archive /Getty Images; pp. 49, 51 Bettmann/Getty Images; p. 53 Bernard Hoffman/The LIFE Picture Collection/Getty Images; p. 55 Corbis Historical/Getty Images; p. 58 Jeffrey Greenberg/Universal Images Group/Getty Images; p. 61 Larry Busacca/Getty Images; interior pages designs (portrait collage) Ollyy/Shutterstock.com, (USA stamp) ducu59us/Shutterstock.com, (fingerprint) Rigamondis /Shutterstock.com, (brochure) Konstanin L/Shutterstock.com, (visa) Sergiy Palamarchuk/Shutterstock.com.

Design: Nelson Sá; Layout: Nicole Russo-Duca;
Photo Researcher: Nicole DiMella